HOW TO DRAW
HORSES

John Green

DOVER PUBLICATIONS, INC.
Mineola, New York

Note

If you'd like to draw pictures of horses, here is a great place to get started! By combining simple shapes and lines, you will discover how to draw a Mustang, a Palomino, a Thoroughbred, and many other breeds (you'll find each horse's name at the bottom of the page).

Each drawing page has between four and six steps. Opposite each group of steps is a Practice Page, which really comes in handy! Be sure to use a pencil with an eraser, so that you can erase lines when needed. For most of the drawings (those showing the entire horse), the first step begins with one or two circles. The circles give an idea of the general shape of the horse's body. In the next steps, you will add a triangular-shaped neck and a mane, as well as the outline and details of the legs, hoofs, and tail. For a few drawings (those showing the horse's head only), you begin with straight and curved lines rather than circles. You then add details to the head.

The last step shows the finished picture of the horse or horse's head. When you have reached this point, you can erase any lines that are not needed. Remember, you can change your drawing until you are pleased with it. Finally, you can go over the lines with a felt-tip pen or a colored marker or pencil. After finishing your drawing, why not color in your pictures of these beautiful horses for some extra fun. Enjoy!

Bibliographical Note

How to Draw Horses is a new work, first published by
Dover Publications, Inc., in 2009.

International Standard Book Number

ISBN-13: 978-0-486-46759-7
ISBN-10: 0-486-46759-7

Manufactured in the United States by LSC Communications
46759709   2020
www.doverpublications.com

HOW TO DRAW
HORSES

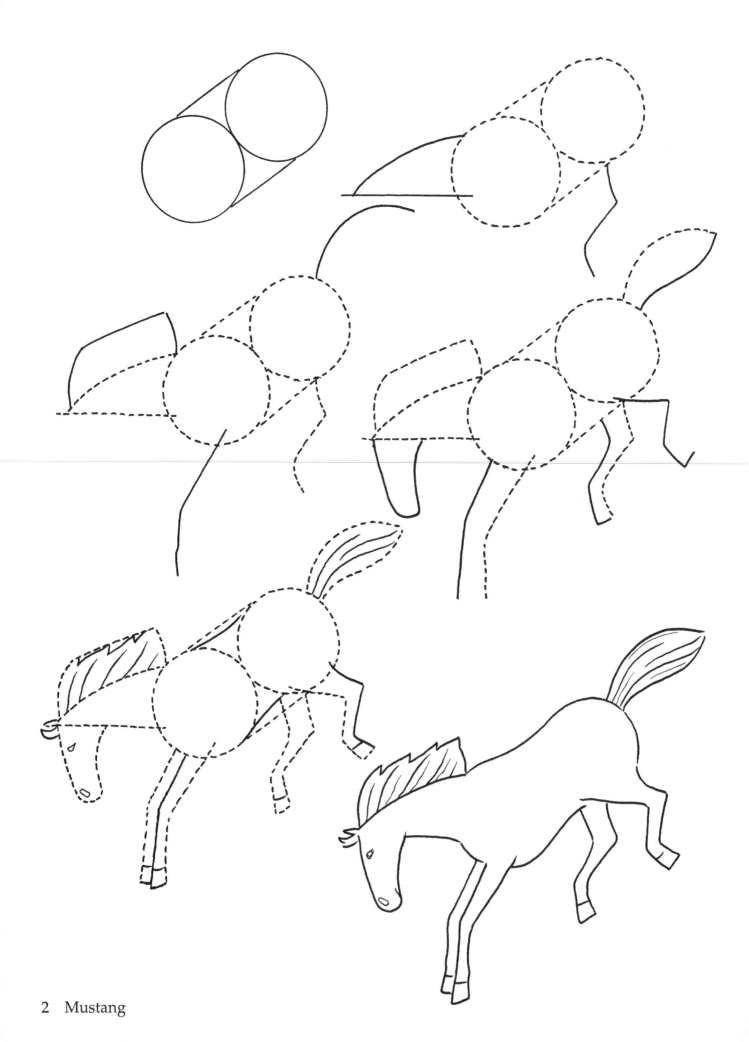

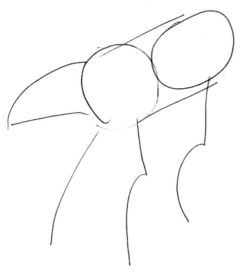

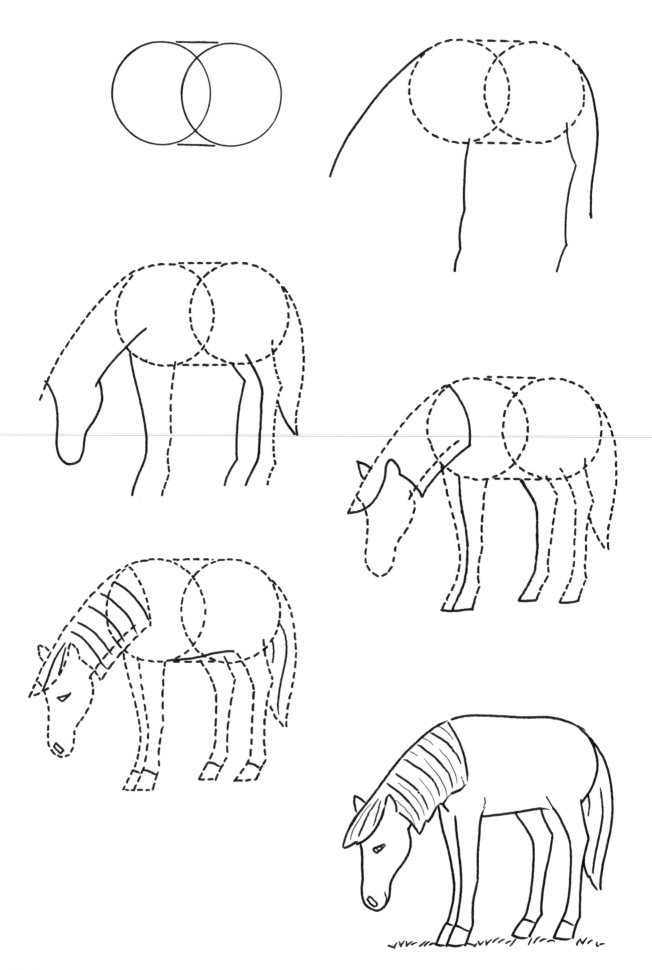

Practice Page

Practice Page

Practice Page

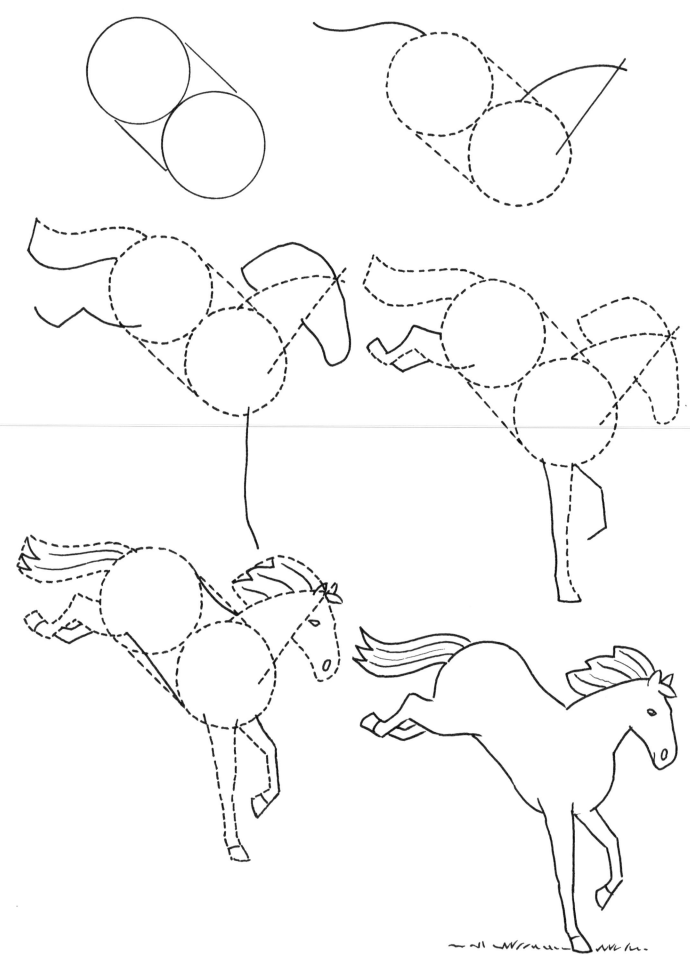

Practice Page

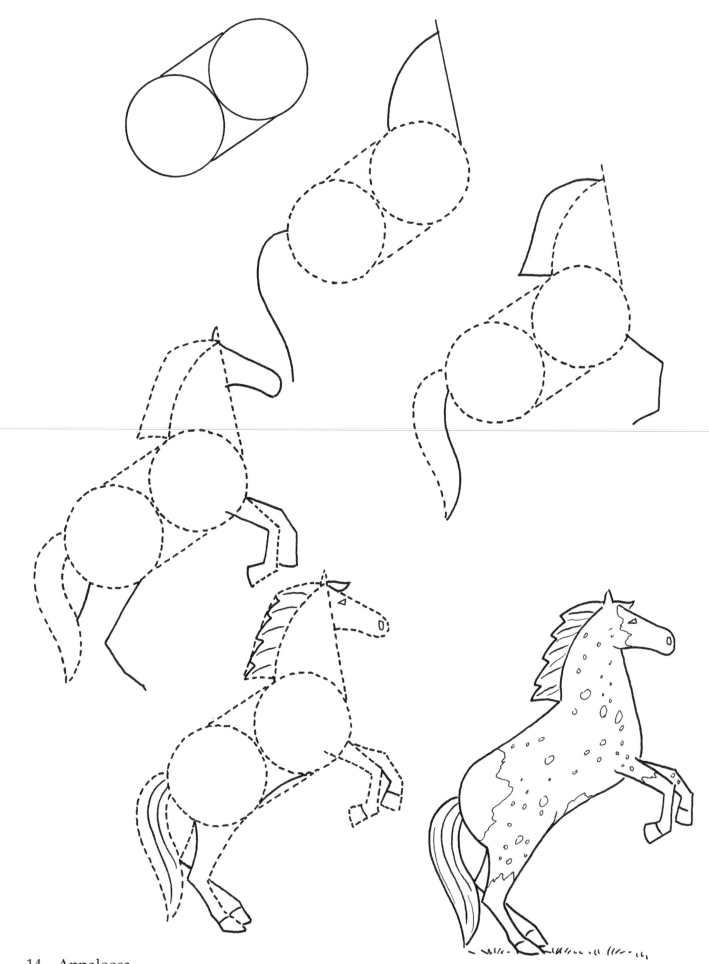

14   Appaloosa

Practice Page

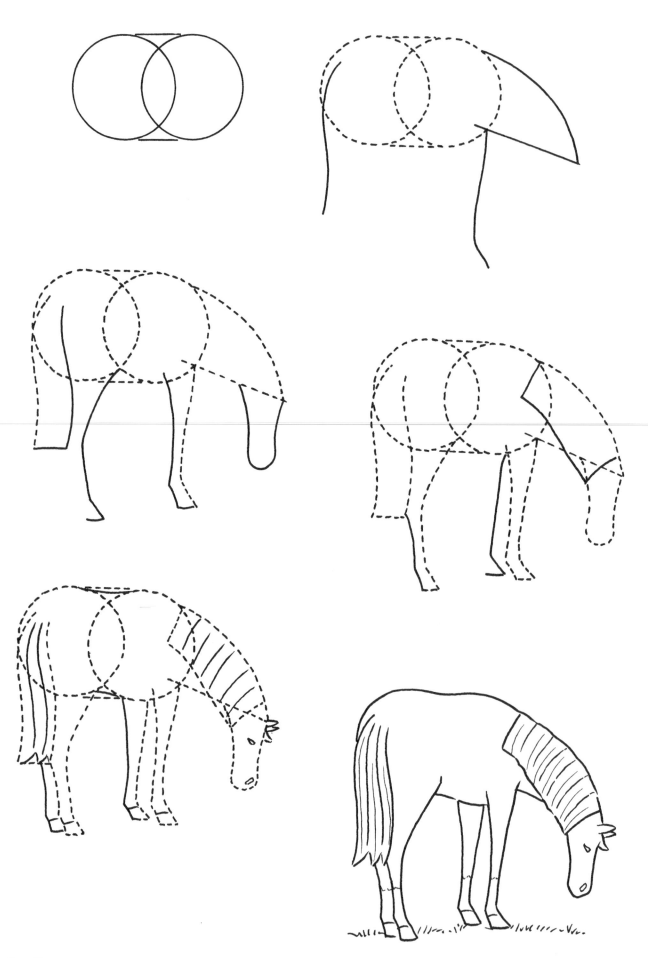

Practice Page

Practice Page

Practice Page

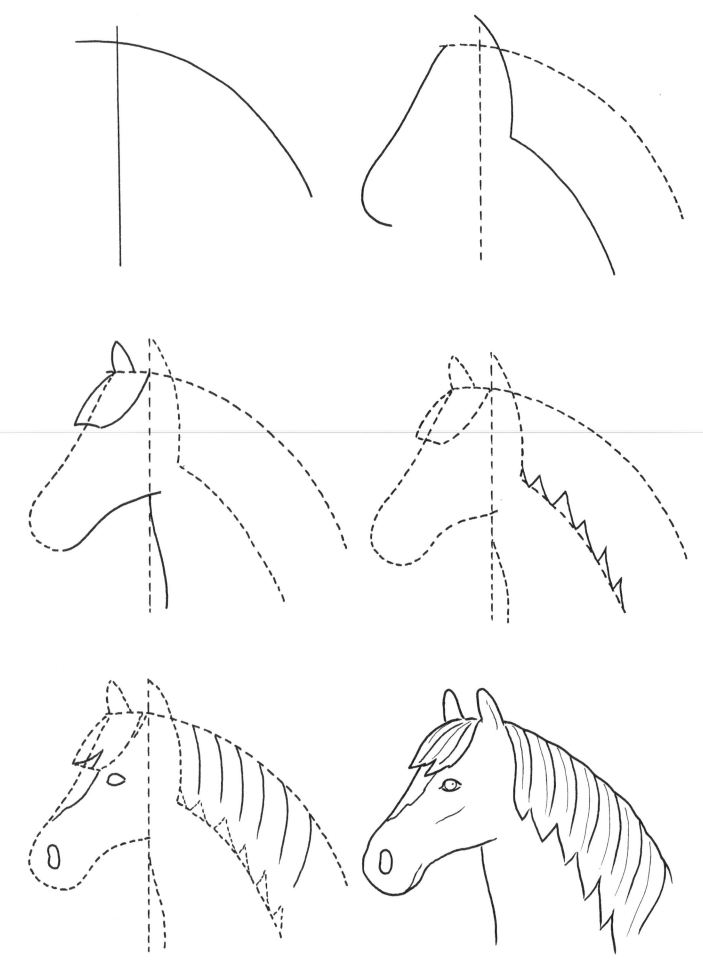

Practice Page

Practice Page

Practice Page

Practice Page

Practice Page

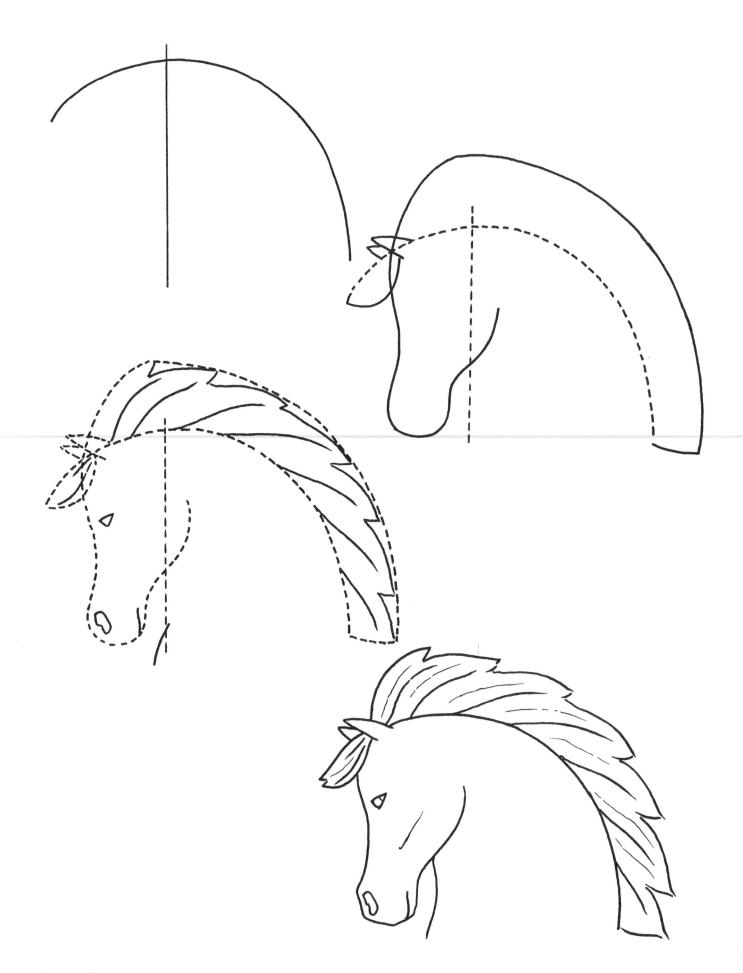

Practice Page

Practice Page

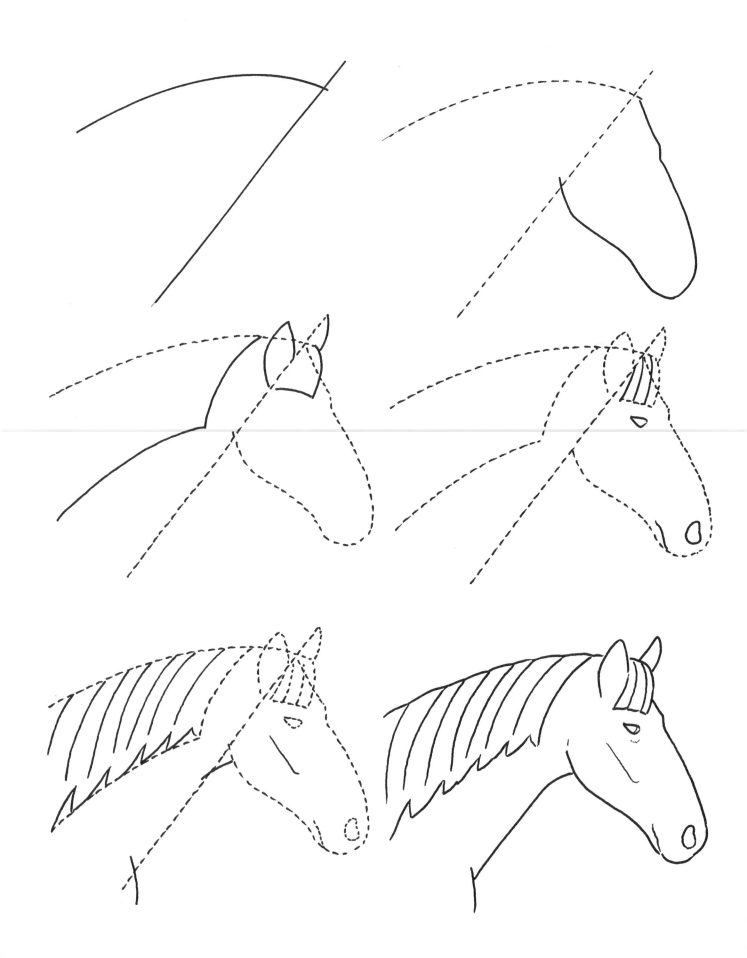

Practice Page

42 Clydesdale

Practice Page

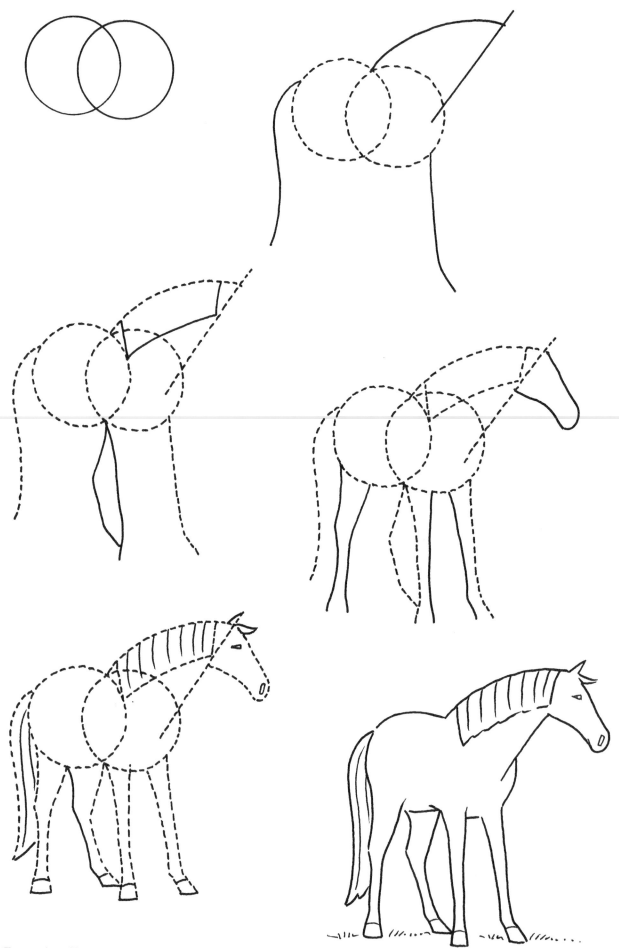

Practice Page

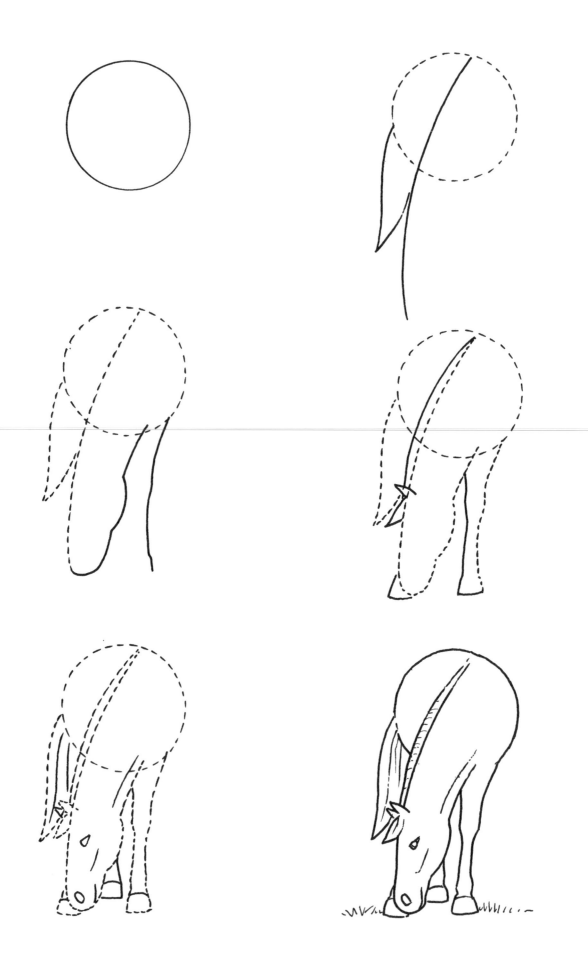

50 Percheron

Practice Page

Practice Page

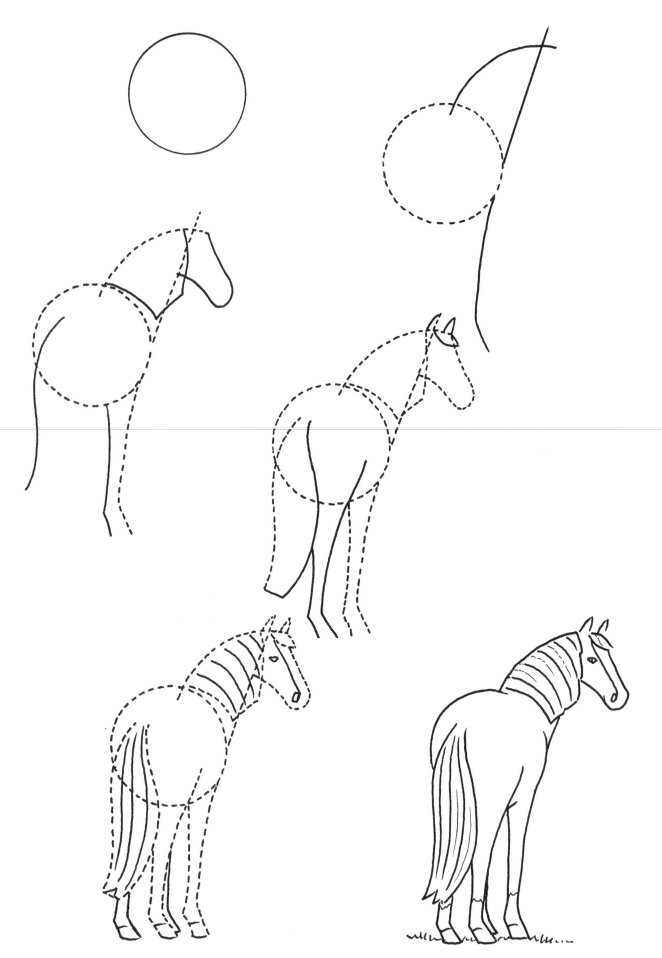

Practice Page

Practice Page .

Practice Page